초등영어 읽기독립

리딩 스타터 2

Reading Starter

재능많은
영어연구소
지음

휴먼
어린이

초등영어 읽기독립 3단계
"28일만 따라 하면 술술 긴 글이 읽혀요!"

리딩 스타터 2 구성

균형적 문해 접근법의 영어 읽기

여러분은 알파벳과 소릿값을 익히고 모음 파닉스를 배워 단어 읽기를 끝낸 후 사이트 워드로 문장 읽기까지 완료했어요. 여기서 나아가 모든 읽기 활동이 의미 있는 것이 되려면 균형적 문해 학습을 해야 해요.

리딩 스타터는 글자와 단어를 읽는 것을 넘어 진정한 읽기의 목적인 글을 읽고 이해하는 단계로 단어와 문장의 사전 지식을 익히고, 그 배경지식을 바탕으로 글의 내용을 이해하고 재확인하는 과정을 가져요.

〈읽기 전 – 읽기 중 – 읽기 후〉의 3단계 읽기

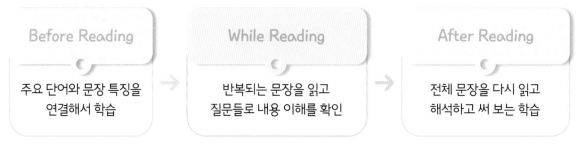

Before Reading	While Reading	After Reading
주요 단어와 문장 특징을 연결해서 학습	반복되는 문장을 읽고 질문들로 내용 이해를 확인	전체 문장을 다시 읽고 해석하고 써 보는 학습

리딩 스타터는 반복되는 문장 패턴을 이용해 그 안의 단어들을 바꿔 새롭게 만들어진 표현들을 담아 글을 구성했어요.
패턴을 이용한 간단한 글이지만 영어로 된 긴 글도 읽을 수 있다는 자신감을 갖게 하는 동시에 반복적이고 다양한 표현들을 통해 단어와 문장의 특징을 자연스럽게 익힐 수 있어요.

또한 초등생이 쉽게 접하는 일상생활의 표현들과 교과 과정에서 배우는 주제 중심 활동을 담은 내용들로 구성되어 쉽게 문장을 이해할 수 있으며, 친숙한 표현들을 통해 영어 읽기에 재미와 흥미를 불러일으켜요.

이렇게 만들었어요!

 매일매일 읽기 독립! 자연스럽게 이루어지는 학습 계획

부담 없는 하루 학습량과 명확하고 목표에 맞는 학습 계획으로 읽기의 성장을 바로바로 확인할 수 있어요. 두 개의 유닛을 끝내고 나면 리뷰와 딕테이션(받아쓰기)을 하며 복습할 수 있어요.

Unit	Grammar	Sentence Pattern
01	명사s	I have eight eyes.
02	There is / There are	There is a pen in my bag.
	Unit 01~02 Review / Dictation	
03	It + 동사s	It tastes salty.
04	can / can't	I can wash my face.
	Unit 03~04 Review / Dictation	
05	on / in / under	It is on the bed.
06	형용사 + 명사	He wears a blue uniform.
	Unit 05~06 Review / Dictation	
07	play (the) + 스포츠/악기	Mia plays soccer.
08	go + 동작ing	She goes biking.
	Unit 07~08 Review / Dictation	
09	Do you + 동사~?	Do you like snow?
10	Does it + 동사~?	Does it have wings?
	Unit 09~10 Review / Dictation	
11	does not + 동사	He does not go to school.
12	am, is, are + 동작ing	She is cooking lunch.
	Unit 11~12 Review / Dictation	
13	명령문	Wake up.
14	will + 동사	It will rain.
	Unit 13~14 Review / Dictation	

• 《리딩 스타터》1, 2권에서 각각 14가지 Grammar와 Sentence Pattern을 배울 수 있어요.

초등영어 읽기독립 3단계

QR코드를 찍으면 오늘 배울 내용을
원어민의 정확한 발음으로 들을 수 있어요!

1 단어 / 문장 미리 보기

글을 읽기 전에 주요 단어와 문장을 미리 보고
글의 내용을 추측해 보며 단어와 문장을 연습해 봐요.

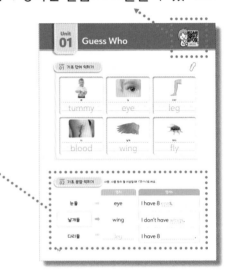

반복되는 문장과 그 문장의 특징을
살펴보고 따라 쓰며 익혀요.

2 본문 읽기

재미있는 일상생활이나 논픽션 등의 주제글을 읽고 글을 이해하는 법을 배워요.

글의 이해를 확인하는 질문들을 통해
역으로 읽는 법을 배울 수 있어요.

이렇게 배워요!

3 한 문장씩 연습하기

배운 기초 단어들과 반복되는 문장으로 이루어진 글을 다시 읽고 전체를 다시 써 보기, 문장 완성하는 연습 등으로 글 읽기에 자신감을 채워 보세요.

반복되는 문장을 다시 쓰다 보면
자연스럽게 문장과 글을 재확인할 수 있어요.

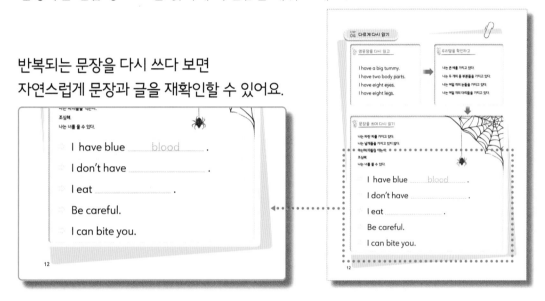

4 리뷰 및 딕테이션

이틀 동안 공부한 두 개의 유닛을 누적 반복하는 연습을 통해 빠르고 정확하게 읽을 수 있어요.
그리고 전체 글을 들으며 딕테이션(받아쓰기)을 할 수 있어요.

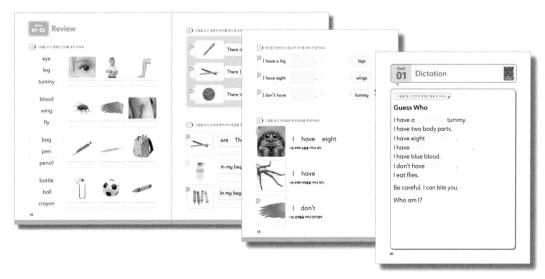

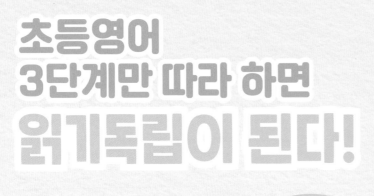

초등영어
3단계만 따라 하면
읽기독립이 된다!

하루 15분

1단계
단어 읽기

파닉스 1, 2

2단계
문장 읽기

사이트 워드

3단계
긴 글 읽기

리딩 스타터 1, 2

1단계 **파닉스 1, 2**　　　　40일만 따라 하면 단어가 읽힌다.

단어 읽기

파닉스 규칙 1
알파벳

파닉스 규칙 2
모음

**파닉스로
낱글자에서 단어 읽기까지!**
파닉스 떼기

파닉스: 알파벳

글자 인지

음가 구별

글자 읽기

1단계 파닉스 알파벳으로 글자 읽기!

파닉스: 모음

단/장모음

이중모음

단어 읽기

1단계 파닉스 모음으로 단어 읽기!

6

사이트 워드

30일만 따라 하면 문장이 읽힌다.

문장 읽기

사이트 워드
단어 뜻과 활용

사이트 워드로 문장 읽기!
사이트 워드 120개, 초등 필수 문장 180개 학습

사이트 워드
단어 활용
초등 표현
문장 읽기

2단계 사이트 워드로 문장 읽기!

리딩 스타터 1, 2

28일만 따라 하면 긴 글이 읽힌다.

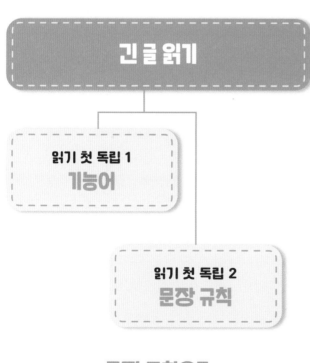

긴 글 읽기

읽기 첫 독립 1
기능어

읽기 첫 독립 2
문장 규칙

**문장 규칙으로
혼자 읽기까지!**
초등 3, 4학년 필수 영단어와 문장 규칙 학습

주제 단어
기능어
문장 규칙
단락 읽기

3단계 기능어로 첫 읽기 도전!

주제 단어
문장 규칙
문장별 확인
단락 이해하기

3단계 문장 규칙으로 첫 읽기 도전!

Part 1

QR코드

배	눈	다리
tummy	eye	leg
피	날개	파리
blood	wing	fly

사람, 사물 등이 둘 이상일 때 <명사s>로 써요.

	명사	명사s
눈들 ➡	eye	I have 8 eyes.
날개들 ➡	wing	I don't have wings.
다리들 ➡	leg	I have 8 _____.

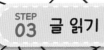

I have a big tummy.
I have two body parts.
I have eight eyes.
I have eight legs.
I have blue blood.
I don't have wings.
I eat flies.

Be careful. I can bite you.

Who am I?

* fly(파리)가 둘 이상일 때 flies로 바꿔 써요.

▶ **Reading Check** | 알맞은 단어를 골라 문장을 완성하세요.

It is about _____.

a	b
a fly	a spider

I have eight _____.

a	b
legs	wings

▶ **Reading Check** | 본문의 내용과 맞으면 Yes, 다르면 No에 표시하세요.

A spider has eight eyes.	☐ YES	☐ NO
A spider has red blood.	☐ YES	☐ NO

11

✌ 영문장을 다시 읽고

I have a big tummy.

I have two body parts.

I have eight eyes.

I have eight legs.

✌ 우리말을 확인하고

나는 큰 배를 가지고 있다.

나는 두 개의 몸 부분들을 가지고 있다.

나는 여덟 개의 눈들을 가지고 있다.

나는 여덟 개의 다리들을 가지고 있다.

✌ 문장을 쓰며 다시 읽기

나는 파란 피를 가지고 있다.

나는 날개들을 가지고 있지 않다.

나는 파리들을 먹는다.

조심해.

나는 너를 물 수 있다.

⟹ I have blue _____blood_____ .

⟹ I don't have _____ .

⟹ I eat _____ .

⟹ Be careful.

⟹ I can bite you.

Unit 02 — In My Bag

QR코드

가방
bag

펜
pen

연필
pencil

병
bottle

공
ball

크레용
crayon

STEP 02 기초 문장 익히기

There is/are ~는 뒤에 오는 명사 수에 따라
〈There is + a 명사〉, 〈There are + 명사s〉로 써요.

한국어	a 명사 l 명사s	There is l There are
펜 한 개	a pen	There is a pen.
연필 두 개	two pencils	There are two pencils.
크레용 네 개	four crayons	

This is my bag.
There is a pen in my bag.
There are two pencils in my bag.

There is a water bottle in my bag.
There are three books in my bag.

There is a ball in my bag.
There are four crayons in my bag.

What do you have in your bag?

▶ **Reading Check |** 알맞은 단어를 골라 문장을 완성하세요.

It is about what is in my _____.

a	b
bag	bottle

There are _____ in my bag.

a	b
a pen	two pencils

▶ **Match |** 문장의 빈칸에 들어갈 알맞은 말을 연결하세요.

There _____ a ball in my bag.   •   •   three books

There are _____ in my bag.   •   •   is

영문장을 다시 읽고

This is my bag.

There is a pen in my bag.

There are two pencils in my bag.

 우리말을 확인하고

이것은 내 가방이다.

내 가방에는 펜 한 개가 있다.

내 가방에는 연필 두 개가 있다.

 문장을 쓰며 다시 읽기

내 가방에는 물병 한 개가 있다.
내 가방에는 책 세 권이 있다.
내 가방에는 공 한 개가 있다.
내 가방에는 크레용 네 개가 있다.
너는 네 가방에 무엇을 가지고 있니?

→ There is a water bottle in my bag.

→ There are three books in my bag.

→ _____ .

→ _____ .

→ What do you have _____ ?

A ▶ 그림을 보고 알맞은 단어를 찾아 쓰세요.

eye
leg
tummy

eye _____ _____

blood
wing
fly

 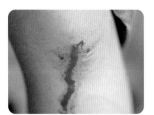

_____ _____ _____

bag
pen
pencil

_____ _____ _____

bottle
ball
crayon

_____ _____ _____

B 그림을 보고 알맞은 단어를 찾아 동그라미 하세요.

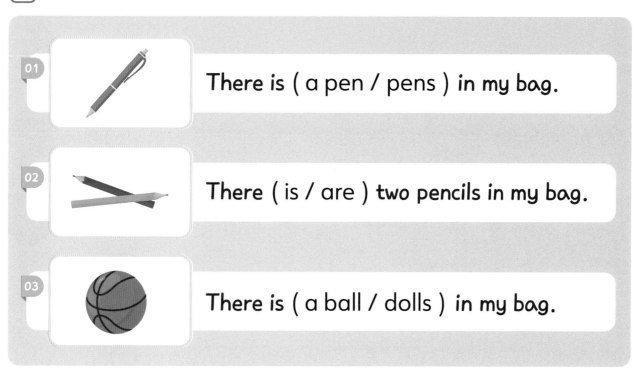

01 There is (a pen / pens) in my bag.

02 There (is / are) two pencils in my bag.

03 There is (a ball / dolls) in my bag.

C 그림을 보고 순서에 맞게 써서 문장을 완성하세요.

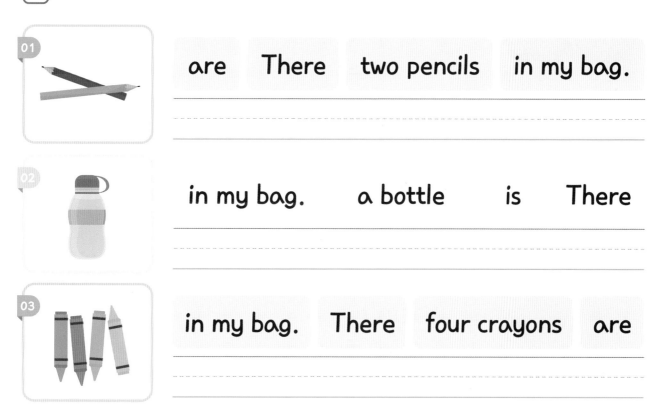

01 are   There   two pencils   in my bag.

02 in my bag.   a bottle   is   There

03 in my bag.   There   four crayons   are

D 문장을 완성하는 데 필요한 단어를 찾아 연결하세요.

01   I have a big   .

02   I have eight   .

03   I don't have   .

legs

wings

tummy

E 그림을 보고 우리말에 맞게 문장을 완성하세요.

01

I   have   eight   .

나는 8개의 눈들을 가지고 있다.

02

I   have   .

나는 8개의 다리들을 가지고 있다.

03

I   don't   .

나는 날개들을 가지고 있지 않다.

Part 2

_____월 _____일 나의 평가는? ☆☆☆☆☆

I Am a Cook

• Unit 03을 끝내고 p.82 Dictation을 하세요.

_____월 _____일 나의 평가는? ☆☆☆☆☆

I Can Do

• Unit 04를 끝내고 p.83 Dictation을 하세요.
• Review를 통해 Unit 03~04를 정리하세요.

요리하다
cook

맛이 나다
taste

(맛이) 짠
salty

굽다
bake

냄새가 나다
smell

채소
vegetable

주어가 it일 때 〈It + 동사s ~〉로 써요.

	동사	It + 동사s
맛이 나다	taste	It tastes salty.
보이다	look	It looks burnt.
냄새가 나다	smell	_____ bad.

I cook dinner.
Oh, no.
It tastes too salty.

I bake bread.
Oh, no.
It looks burnt.

I make soup.
Oh, no.
It smells bad.

Don't worry, Matt.
We can eat vegetables.

* burnt는 '(불에) 탄'이라는 뜻이에요.

▶ Reading Check | 본문의 내용과 맞으면 Yes에, 다르면 No에 표시하세요.

Matt cooks dinner.	◯ YES	◯ NO
Soup smells bad.	◯ YES	◯ NO

▶ Match | 그림과 어울리는 문장을 연결하세요.

•

It looks burnt.

•

It tastes too salty.

영문장을 다시 읽고

I cook dinner.
It tastes too salty.
I bake bread.
It looks burnt.

 우리말을 확인하고

나는 저녁을 요리한다.

그것은 너무 짠 맛이 난다.

나는 빵을 굽는다.

그것은 타 보인다.

 문장을 쓰며 다시 읽기

나는 수프를 만든다.
그것은 나쁜 냄새가 난다.
걱정하지 마, 매트.
우리는 채소를 먹을 수 있어.

 I _____ make soup _____ .

 It _____ bad.

 _____ Don't worry, Matt _____ .

 We can _____ eat vegetables _____ .

QR코드

STEP 01 기초 단어 익히기

침대

bed

씻다

wash

얼굴

face

식탁을 차리다

set the table

돕다

help

접시

dish

STEP 02 기초 문장 익히기

'할 수 있다'는 〈can + 동사〉, '할 수 없다'는 〈can't + 동사〉로 써요.

동사구	can + 동사구
얼굴을 씻을 수 있다 ➡ wash my face	I can wash my face.
설거지를 할 수 있다 ➡ do the dishes	I can do the dishes.
엄마를 도울 수 있다 ➡ help my mom	I _____.

I am grown up now.
I am not a baby.

I can make my bed.
I can wash my face.
I can eat vegetables.

I can help my mom.
I can set the table.
I can do the dishes.

Oh, my.
I can't do everything well.

▶ Reading Check | 본문의 내용과 맞으면 Yes, 다르면 No에 표시하세요.

I can't wash my face.	☐ YES ☐ NO
I can wash the dishes.	☐ YES ☐ NO

▶ Match | 그림과 어울리는 문장을 연결하세요.

•   •   I can make my bed.

•   •   I can set the table.

24

✌ 영문장을 다시 읽고

I am grown up now.

I am not a baby.

I can make my bed.

I can wash my face.

I can eat vegetables.

✌ 우리말을 확인하고

나는 이제 다 컸다.

나는 아기가 아니다.

나는 침대를 정리할 수 있다.

나는 세수를 할 수 있다.

나는 채소를 먹을 수 있다.

✌ 문장을 쓰며 다시 읽기

나는 엄마를 도울 수 있다.
나는 식탁을 차릴 수 있다.
나는 설거지를 할 수 있다.
나는 모든 것을 잘할 수 없다.

→ I ____ can help my mom ____ .

→ I _____ .

→ I _____ .

→ I ____ everything well .

A ▶ 그림을 보고 알맞은 단어를 찾아 쓰세요.

cook
taste
salty

cook

bake
smell
vegetable

bed
wash
face

set the table
help
dish

B ▶ 그림을 보고 알맞은 단어를 찾아 동그라미 하세요.

01 It (taste / tastes) too salty.

02 It (looks / look) burnt.

03 It (smell / smells) bad.

C ▶ 그림을 보고 순서에 맞게 써서 문장을 완성하세요.

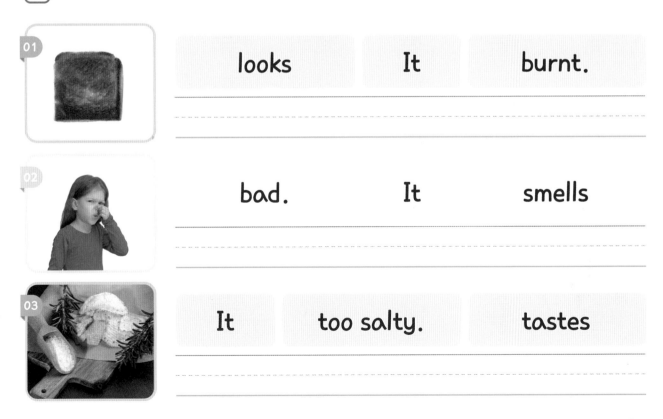

01 looks   It   burnt.

02 bad.   It   smells

03 It   too salty.   tastes

문장을 완성하는 데 필요한 단어를 찾아 연결하세요.

01 I can _____ my mom. •

02 I can _____ the dishes. •

03 I can _____ my face. •

• wash

• do

• help

E 그림을 보고 우리말에 맞게 문장을 완성하세요.

01 I can _____ .

나는 세수를 할 수 있다.

02 I can _____ .

나는 설거지를 할 수 있다.

03 I _____ .

나는 엄마를 도울 수 있다.

28

Part 3

Unit 05

_____월 _____일

나의 평가는?
☆ ☆ ☆ ☆ ☆

Where Is It?

• Unit 05를 끝내고 p.84 Dictation을 하세요.

Unit 06

_____월 _____일

나의 평가는?
☆ ☆ ☆ ☆ ☆

His Job

• Unit 06을 끝내고 p.85 Dictation을 하세요.
• Review를 통해 Unit 05~06을 정리하세요.

Where Is It?

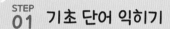

STEP 01 기초 단어 익히기

밖에

outside

코트

coat

장갑

glove

주머니

pocket

눈사람

snowman

단추

button

STEP 02 기초 문장 익히기   물건이 어디에 있는지 위치를 말할 때 〈on, in, under〉를 써요.

전치사	on | in | under
침대 위에 → on	It is on the bed.
너의 주머니 안에 → in	They are in your pocket.
나무 아래에 → under	It is _____ the tree.

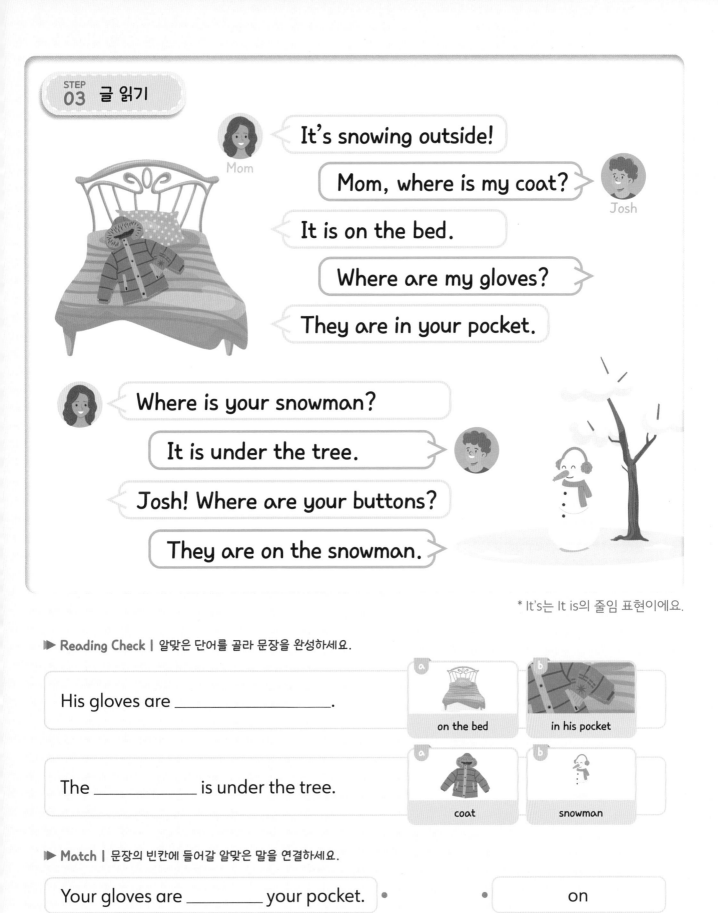

It's snowing outside!

Mom

Mom, where is my coat?

Josh

It is on the bed.

Where are my gloves?

They are in your pocket.

Where is your snowman?

It is under the tree.

Josh! Where are your buttons?

They are on the snowman.

* It's는 It is의 줄임 표현이에요.

▶ **Reading Check** | 알맞은 단어를 골라 문장을 완성하세요.

His gloves are _____.

a. on the bed
b. in his pocket

The _____ is under the tree.

a. coat
b. snowman

▶ **Match** | 문장의 빈칸에 들어갈 알맞은 말을 연결하세요.

Your gloves are _____ your pocket. •   • on

Your coat is _____ the bed. •   • in

☝ 영문장을 다시 읽고

It's snowing outside!
Mom, where is my coat?
It is **on the bed**.
Where are my gloves?
They are **in your pocket**.

✌ 우리말을 확인하고

밖에 눈이 오고 있어.
엄마, 내 코트는 어디에 있어요?
그것은 **침대 위에 있어**.
내 장갑은 어디에 있어요?
그것들은 **너의 주머니 안에 있어**.

🖐 문장을 쓰며 다시 읽기

네 눈사람은 어디에 있니?
그것은 **나무 아래에 있어요**.
네 단추들은 어디에 있니?
그것들은 **눈사람에 있어요**.

→ Where _____ is your snowman _____ ?

→ It is _____ .

→ Where _____ are your buttons _____ ?

→ They _____ .

QR코드

홀륭한
_____
great

직업
_____
job

제복, 교복
_____
uniform

필요하다
_____
need

찾다
_____
find

입다
_____
wear

STEP
02 기초 문장 익히기   크기, 상태, 색 등을 나타내는 형용사는 〈형용사 + 명사〉로 써요.

		형용사	형용사 + 명사
훌륭한 직업	➡	great	a great job
파란 제복	➡	blue	a blue uniform
어린 여자아이	➡	little	a _____ girl

Tim has a great job.
He is a police officer.
He wears a blue uniform.
He works at the police station.

Tim always helps people.
Today, a little girl needs his help.
He finds her dog.
She is very happy with his help.
He is her superhero.

▶ Reading Check | 알맞은 단어를 골라 문장을 완성하세요.

It is about the _____.

a police officer

b superman

Tim has a _____ job.

a blue

b great

▶ Match | 문장의 빈칸에 들어갈 알맞은 말을 연결하세요.

Tim helps a _____ . •

Tim wears a _____ . •

• blue uniform

• little girl

✌ 영문장을 다시 읽고

Tim has a great job.

He is a police officer.

He wears a blue uniform.

He works at the police station.

✌ 우리말을 확인하고

팀은 훌륭한 직업이 있다.

그는 경찰관이다.

그는 파란 제복을 입는다.

그는 경찰서에서 일한다.

✌ 문장을 쓰며 다시 읽기

팀은 항상 사람들을 돕는다.
오늘, 어린 여자아이가 그의 도움을 필요로 한다.
그는 그녀의 개를 찾는다.
그녀는 그의 도움으로 매우 행복하다.
그는 그녀의 영웅이다.

→ **Tim** <u>always helps people</u> .

→ **Today,** _____ <u>needs his help</u> .

→ **He** _____ .

→ **She** <u>is very happy with his help</u> .

→ **He** <u>is her superhero</u> .

Unit 05~06 Review

A ▶ 그림을 보고 알맞은 단어를 찾아 쓰세요.

coat
glove
outside

coat _____ _____

pocket
button
snowman

_____ _____ _____

great
job
uniform

_____ _____ _____

wear
need
find

_____ _____ _____

36

B 그림을 보고 알맞은 단어를 찾아 동그라미 하세요.

01   It is (on / in) the bed.

02   They are (in / under) your pocket.

03   It is (on / under) the tree.

C 그림을 보고 순서에 맞게 써서 문장을 완성하세요.

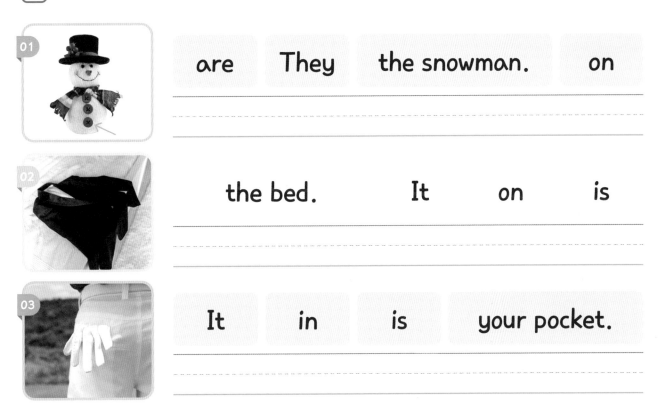

01   are   They   the snowman.   on

02   the bed.   It   on   is

03   It   in   is   your pocket.

D ▸ 문장을 완성하는 데 필요한 단어를 찾아 연결하세요.

01 Tim has a _____ .

02 He wears a _____ .

03 A _____ needs his help.

little girl

great job

blue uniform

E ▸ 그림을 보고 우리말에 맞게 문장을 완성하세요.

01 Tim has a _____ .

팀은 훌륭한 직업이 있다.

02 He wears a _____ .

그는 파란 제복을 입는다.

03 A _____ needs his help .

어린 여자아이는 그의 도움을 필요로 한다.

Part 4

Unit 07

____월 ____일

나의 평가는?
☆☆☆☆☆

Sports and Music

• Unit 07을 끝내고 p.86 Dictation을 하세요.

Unit 08

____월 ____일

나의 평가는?
☆☆☆☆☆

Go Camping

• Unit 08를 끝내고 p.87 Dictation을 하세요.
• Review를 통해 Unit 07~08을 정리하세요.

QR코드

STEP 01 기초 단어 익히기

축구	야구	농구
soccer	baseball	basketball

피아노	바이올린	첼로
piano	violin	cello

STEP 02 기초 문장 익히기

'스포츠를 하다'는 〈play + 스포츠〉, '악기를 연주하다'는 〈play + the 악기〉를 써요.

	스포츠	악기	play + 스포츠	the 악기
축구를 하다 ➡	soccer	play soccer
야구를 하다 ➡	baseball	play baseball
피아노를 연주하다 ➡	piano	the ___

My friends play sports every evening.
Mia plays soccer.
Jack plays baseball.
Sue plays basketball.

My family has music time every evening.
My dad plays the piano.
My mom plays the violin.
My sister plays the cello.

I love reading books.
I do not like sports or music.

▶ **Reading Check** | 본문의 내용과 맞으면 Yes, 다르면 No에 표시하세요.

My family loves sports.	☐ YES	☐ NO
Mia plays basketball every evening.	☐ YES	☐ NO

▶ **Match** | 그림과 어울리는 문장을 연결하세요.

   •   •   My dad plays the piano.

   •   •   Jack plays baseball.

✌️ 영문장을 다시 읽고

My friends play sports every evening.
Mia plays soccer.
Jack plays baseball.
Sue plays basketball.

✌️ 우리말을 확인하고

내 친구들은 매일 저녁에 운동을 한다.
미아는 **축구를 한다.**
잭은 **야구를 한다.**
수는 **농구를 한다.**

✌️ 문장을 쓰며 다시 읽기

내 가족은 매일 저녁에 음악 시간을 갖는다.
아빠는 피아노를 연주한다.
엄마는 바이올린을 연주한다.
여동생은 첼로를 연주한다.
나는 책을 읽는 것을 좋아한다.

→ **My family** has music time every evening .

→ **My dad** plays the piano .

→ **My mom** _____ .

→ **My sister** _____ .

→ I love reading books .

Go Camping

야영하다
camp

자전거를 타다
bike

잡다
catch

하이킹하다
hike

구름
cloud

불 옆에
by the fire

'~하러 가다' 라고 말할 때 〈go + 동작 ing〉로 써요.

	동작	go + 동작 ing
하이킹하러 가다	hike	go hiking
자전거 타러 가다	bike	go biking
야영하러 가다	camp	

Ella goes camping with her mom and dad.
She goes biking and catches a butterfly.
Her dad goes fishing and catches a fish.
Her mom goes hiking and sees clouds.

At night, they sit by the fire.
They go looking at the sky and see the stars.

▶ Reading Check | 알맞은 단어를 골라 문장을 완성하세요.

It is about _____.

a camping
b family

Ella goes _____.

a biking
b cooking

▶ Match | 문장의 빈칸에 들어갈 알맞은 말을 연결하세요.

Her dad goes _____ and catches a fish. •   • fishing

Her mom goes _____ and sees clouds. •   • hiking

44

✌ 영문장을 다시 읽고

Ella **goes camping** with
her mom and dad.
She **goes biking**
and catches a butterfly.
Her dad **goes fishing** and
catches a fish.

✌ 우리말을 확인하고

엘라는 그녀의 엄마, 아빠와
야영하러 간다.
그녀는 **자전거 타러 가고**
나비를 잡는다.
그녀의 아빠는 **낚시하러 가고**
물고기를 잡는다.

✌ 문장을 쓰며 다시 읽기

그녀의 엄마는 **하이킹하러 가고**
구름을 본다.
밤에 그들은 불 옆에 앉는다.
그들은 **하늘을 보러 가고**
별을 본다.

→ Her mom _____
and ___*sees clouds*___ .

→ At night, they ___*sit by the fire*___ .

→ They _____ the sky
and ___*see the stars*___ .

45

Review

그림을 보고 알맞은 단어를 찾아 쓰세요.

soccer
baseball
basketball

 soccer _____ _____

piano
violin
cello

_____ _____ _____

camp
hike
bike

_____ _____ _____

catch
cloud
by the fire

_____ _____ _____

그림을 보고 알맞은 단어를 찾아 동그라미 하세요.

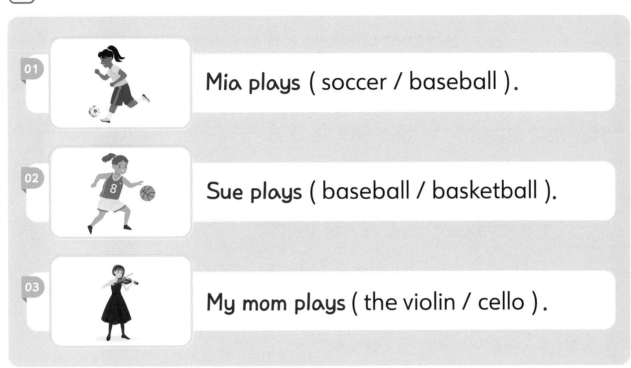

01 Mia plays (soccer / baseball).

02 Sue plays (baseball / basketball).

03 My mom plays (the violin / cello).

C 그림을 보고 순서에 맞게 써서 문장을 완성하세요.

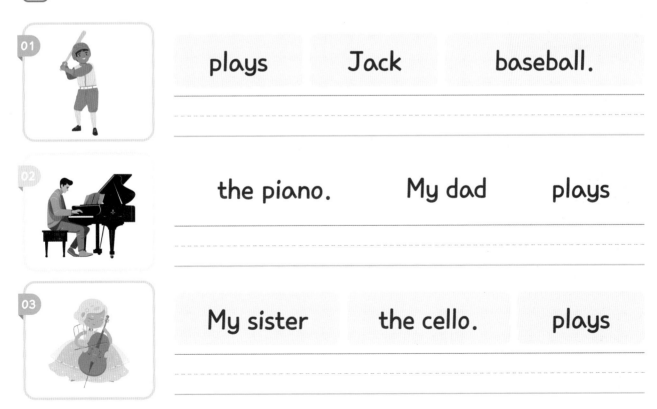

01 plays   Jack   baseball.

02 the piano.   My dad   plays

03 My sister   the cello.   plays

문장을 완성하는데 필요한 단어를 찾아 연결하세요.

01 Ella goes   .   ·   biking

02 Her dad goes   .   ·   hiking

03 Her mom goes   .   ·   fishing

E 그림을 보고 우리말에 맞게 문장을 완성하세요.

01

Ella   goes

with her mom and dad   .

엘라는 그녀의 엄마, 아빠와 야영하러 간다.

02

Her   dad   .

그녀의 아빠는 낚시하러 간다.

03

They   at

the sky   .

그들은 하늘을 보러 간다.

Part 5

Unit 09

_____ 월 _____ 일

나의 평가는?
☆ ☆ ☆ ☆ ☆

Do You Like Snow?

• Unit 09를 끝내고 p.88 Dictation을 하세요.

Unit 10

_____ 월 _____ 일

나의 평가는?
☆ ☆ ☆ ☆ ☆

Does It Have Wings?

• Unit 10을 끝내고 p.89 Dictation을 하세요.
• Review를 통해 Unit 09~10을 정리하세요.

QR코드

STEP 01 기초 단어 익히기

떨어지다
fall

놀다
play

젖은, 축축한
wet

무지개
rainbow

색깔
color

예쁜
pretty

STEP 02 기초 문장 익히기

질문을 할 때 문장 앞에 Do을 써서 〈Do you~?〉로 질문해요.

동사구	Do you + 동사구?
눈을 좋아하다 ➡ like snow	Do you like snow?
비를 좋아하다 ➡ like rain	Do you like rain?
무지개를 좋아하다 ➡ like rainbows	

Jane: Snow is falling from the sky.
Do you like snow, Matt?

Matt: Yes, I do. I like to play in the snow.

Jane: How about rain?
Do you like rain?

Matt: No, I don't. It is too wet outside.
But I like rainbows.
Do you like rainbows?

Jane: Yes, I do. They are so pretty.

Matt: I love the colors.

▶ **Reading Check** | 본문의 내용과 맞으면 Yes, 다르면 No에 표시하세요.

Matt likes snow.	◯ YES	◯ NO
Matt does not like rainbows.	◯ YES	◯ NO

▶ **Match** | 질문에 알맞은 대답과 연결하세요.

Do you like snow, Matt?　　•　　•　No, I don't.

Do you like rain, Matt?　　•　　•　Yes, I do.

✌ 영문장을 다시 읽고

Snow is falling from the sky.

Do you like snow, Matt?

Yes, I do. I like to play in the snow.

How about rain?

Do you like rain?

✌ 우리말을 확인하고

눈이 하늘에서 내리고 있어.

너는 눈을 좋아하니, 매트?

응, 맞아. 나는 눈에서 노는 게 좋아.

비는 어때?

너는 비를 좋아하니?

✌ 문장을 쓰며 다시 읽기

아니, 그렇지 않아. 밖이 너무 습해.

하지만 나는 무지개는 좋아.

너는 무지개를 좋아하니?

응, 맞아. 그것들은 너무 예뻐.

나는 그 색깔들을 좋아해.

→ No, _____ . It is too wet outside .

→ But I _____ like rainbows _____ .

→ _____ ?

→ Yes, _____ . They are so pretty .

→ I _____ love the colors _____ .

퀴즈

quiz

깃털

feather

날다

fly

수영하다

swim

살다

live

추운 곳

cold place

주어가 It일 때 문장 앞에 Does를 써서 〈Does it ~?〉으로 질문해요.

	동사구	Does it + 동사구?
날개가 있다	have wing	Does it have wings?
수영을 잘하다	swim well	Does it swim well?
날다	fly	

Jane: It's time for a quiz.

Matt: Does it have wings?

Jane: Yes, it does.
It has black and white feathers.

Matt: Does it fly?

Jane: No, it doesn't.

Matt: Does it swim well?

Jane: Yes. It swims with its wings.

Matt: Does it live in a cold place?

Jane: Yes, it does.
Do you know what it is?

▶ **Reading Check** | 알맞은 단어를 골라 문장을 완성하세요.

It is about a _____ .

a dolphin   b penguin

It lives in a _____ .

a cold place   b hot place

▶ **Match** | 질문에 알맞은 대답과 연결하세요.

Does it fly?   •   •   No, it doesn't.

Does it swim well?   •   •   Yes, it does.

54

영문장을 다시 읽고

It's time for a quiz.
Does it have wings?
Yes, it does.
It has black and white feathers.

 우리말을 확인하고

퀴즈 시간이야.
그것은 날개가 있니?
응, 맞아.
그것은 검은색과 흰색의 깃털이 있어.

✌ 문장을 쓰며 다시 읽기

그것은 날 수 있니?
아니, 그렇지 않아.
그것은 수영을 잘하니?
맞아. 그것은 날개로 수영을 해.
그것은 추운 지역에 사니?
응, 맞아. 너는 그것이 무엇인지 아니?

 Does _____it fly_____ ?

 No, _____ .

 _____ ?

 Yes. _____It swims with its wings_____ .

 _____ ?

Yes, it does. Do you know what it is?

Review

A ▶ 그림을 보고 알맞은 단어를 찾아 쓰세요.

fall
play
wet

_____ fall _____   _____   _____

rainbow
color
pretty

quiz
feather
fly

swim
live
cold place

그림을 보고 알맞은 단어를 찾아 동그라미 하세요.

01 (Do / Does) it have wings?

02 Does (it / they) fly?

03 (It does / Does it) swim well?

C 그림을 보고 순서에 맞게 써서 문장을 완성하세요.

01 it   Does   swim well?

_____

02 fly?   it   Does

_____

03 it   have wings?   Does

_____

문장을 읽고 알맞은 그림을 찾아 연결하세요.

01 Do you like rainbows?   •

02 Do you like snow?   •

03 Do you like rain?   •

E 그림을 보고 우리말에 맞게 문장을 완성하세요.

01

Do   you   ?

너는 무지개를 좋아하니?

02

Do   you   ?

너는 비를 좋아하니?

03

Do   ?

너는 눈을 좋아하니?

Part 6

Unit 11

_____월 _____일

나의 평가는?
☆☆☆☆☆

My Little Brother

• Unit 11을 끝내고 p.90 Dictation을 하세요.

Unit 12

_____월 _____일

나의 평가는?
☆☆☆☆☆

What Are You Doing?

• Unit 12를 끝내고 p.91 Dictation을 하세요.
• Review를 통해 Unit 11~12를 정리하세요.

My Little Brother

QR코드

남자형제 (형, 남동생)

brother

학교에 가다

go to school

숙제

homework

청소하다

clean

방

room

간식

snack

주어가 'He, She' 등일 때 '~하지 않는다' 의미는 〈does not + 동사〉로 써요.

	동사	does not + 동사
학교에 가지 않는다	go to school	He does not go to school.
숙제를 하지 않는다	do his homework	He does not do his homework.
방을 청소하지 않는다	clean his room	He _____.

60

I go to school.
My brother does not go to school.
I do my homework.
He does not do his homework.
I clean my room.
He does not clean his room.

My brother takes my toys.
He eats my snacks.

I like him.
But I am not happy with him.

* does not의 줄임 표현은 doesn't로 써요.

▶ **Reading Check** | 본문의 내용과 맞으면 Yes, 다르면 No에 표시하세요.

| The story is about my toy. | ☐ YES | ☐ NO |
| My brother doesn't take my toys. | ☐ YES | ☐ NO |

▶ **Match** | 그림과 어울리는 문장을 연결하세요.

•

My brother doesn't go to school.

•

My brother doesn't clean his room.

61

✌ 영문장을 다시 읽고

I go to school.
My brother does not go to school.
I do my homework.
He does not do his homework.

✌ 우리말을 확인하고

나는 학교에 간다.

내 남동생은 학교에 가지 않는다.

나는 내 숙제를 한다.

그는 그의 숙제를 하지 않는다.

✌ 문장을 쓰며 다시 읽기

나는 내 방을 청소한다.
그는 그의 방을 청소하지 않는다.
내 남동생은 내 장난감을 가져간다.
그는 내 간식을 먹는다.
나는 그를 좋아한다. 하지만 나는 그와 함께 행복하지 않다.

→ I _____clean my room_____ .

→ He _____ .

→ My brother _____takes my toys_____ .

→ He _____eats my snacks_____ .

→ I like him . But I am not happy with him.

What Are You Doing?

QR코드

부엌

kitchen

점심

lunch

거실

living room

보다

watch

자다

sleep

바쁜

busy

지금 하고 있는 진행 중인 일은 〈am, is, are + 동작ing〉로 써요.

동사구	am, is, are + 동작ing
점심을 요리하고 있다 ➡ cook lunch	I am cooking lunch.
TV를 보고 있다 ➡ watch TV	He is watching TV.
책을 읽고 있다 ➡ read a book	You are _____ .

Today is Sunday.
Dad is in the kitchen.
He is cooking lunch.
Mom is in the living room.
She is watching TV.
My sister is in the bathroom.
She is washing a dog.

I am in my room.
I am reading a book.
I am not sleeping.
I am busy, too.

▶ Reading Check | 본문의 내용과 맞으면 Yes, 다르면 No에 표시하세요.

My dad is watching TV.	☐ YES ☐ NO
I am sleeping in my room.	☐ YES ☐ NO

▶ Match | 그림과 어울리는 문장을 연결하세요.

• My dad is cooking lunch.

• My sister is washing a dog.

영문장을 다시 읽고

Today is Sunday.
Dad is in the kitchen.
He is cooking lunch.
Mom is in the living room.
She is watching TV.

우리말을 확인하고

오늘은 일요일이다.
아빠는 부엌에 있다.
그는 점심을 요리하고 있다.
엄마는 거실에 있다.
그녀는 TV를 보고 있다.

문장을 쓰며 다시 읽기

내 여동생은 욕실에 있다.
그녀는 개를 씻기고 있다.
나는 내 방에 있다.
나는 책을 읽고 있다.
나는 자고 있지 않다. 나도 바쁘다.

→ My sister ___is in the bathroom___ .

→ She _____ ___a dog___ .

→ I ___am in my room___ .

→ I _____ ___a book___ .

→ I ___am not sleeping___ . I am busy, too.

A 그림을 보고 알맞은 단어를 찾아 쓰세요.

brother
homework
go to school

brother

clean
room
snack

kitchen
lunch
living room

watch
sleep
busy

그림을 보고 알맞은 단어를 찾아 동그라미 하세요.

01 My brother (do not / does not) go to school.

02 He does not (do / go) his homework.

03 He does not (do / clean) his room.

C 그림을 보고 순서에 맞게 써서 문장을 완성하세요.

01 | does not | do | He | his homework. |

02 | He | clean | his room. | does not |

03 | does not | to school. | go | My brother |

D ▶ 문장을 완성하는 데 필요한 단어를 찾아 연결하세요.

01 I am   a book.   •

02 He is   lunch.   •

03 She is   a dog.   •

• washing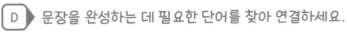

• reading

• cooking

E ▶ 그림을 보고 우리말에 맞게 문장을 완성하세요.

01

She   is   .

그녀는 개를 씻기고 있다.

02

He   is   .

그는 점심을 요리하고 있다.

03

I   a   .

나는 책을 읽고 있다.

Part 7

Go to School

• Unit 13을 끝내고 p.92 Dictation을 하세요.

The Weather

• Unit 14를 끝내고 p.93 Dictation을 하세요.
• Review를 통해 Unit 13~14를 정리하세요.

STEP 01 기초 단어 익히기

일어나다
wake up

늦은
late

잊다
forget

입다
put on

가져오다
bring

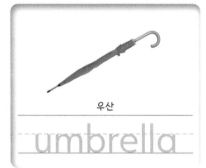
우산
umbrella

STEP 02 기초 문장 익히기

'~해라'라고 말할 때는 문장을 동사로 시작하고, 동사의 첫 글자는 대문자로 써요.

		동사	명령문
일어나다	➡	wake up	Wake up .
입다	➡	put on	Put on your coat .
가져오다	➡	bring	_____ your umbrella.

It is 7 o'clock.
Wake up, Sue.
It is too late.
Take your lunch box.
Don't forget your bag.

It is cold outside.
Put on your coat.
Oh, my. It is raining.
Bring your umbrella.

▶ **Reading Check |** 본문의 내용과 맞으면 Yes, 다르면 No에 표시하세요.

It is a rainy day.	☐ YES	☐ NO
Sue forgets her bag.	☐ YES	☐ NO

▶ **Match |** 그림과 어울리는 문장을 연결하세요.

- Take your lunch box.

- Bring your umbrella.

71

영문장을 다시 읽고

It is 7 o'clock.
Wake up, Sue.
It is too late.
Take your lunch box.

 우리말을 확인하고

7시이다.
일어나라, 수.
너무 늦었다.
점심 도시락을 가져가라.

 문장을 쓰며 다시 읽기

네 가방을 잊지 마라.
밖이 춥다.
네 겉옷을 입어라.
비가 오고 있다.
우산을 가져와라.

→ Don't _____forget your bag_____ .

→ It _____is cold outside_____ .

→ _____ .

→ It _____is raining_____ .

→ _____ .

72

STEP 01 기초 단어 익히기

어두운	구름	오후
dark	cloud	afternoon

숨바꼭질	~안에	재미
hide and seek	inside	fun

STEP 02 기초 문장 익히기

앞으로 할 일이나 일어날 일은 〈will + 동사〉로 말해요.

	동사	will + 동사
비가 올 것이다	rain	It will rain.
놀 것이다	play	I will play.
눈이 올 것이다	snow	It _____ .

73

Do you see the dark clouds?
It will rain in the afternoon.
I will play inside the house.

Tomorrow will be sunny.
We can go to the park.
Let's play hide and seek.

From Tuesday to Friday, it will snow.
Wear gloves and a scarf.
Let's have fun in the snow.

▶ **Reading Check** | 알맞은 단어를 골라 문장을 완성하세요.

It is about the _____.

a weather   b park

It will be _____ tomorrow.

a sunny   b rainy

▶ **Match** | 문장의 빈칸에 들어갈 알맞은 말을 연결하세요.

It _____ rain in the afternoon. •   • will

Tomorrow _____ sunny. •   • will be

74

✌ 영문장을 다시 읽고

Do you see the dark clouds?
It will rain in the afternoon.
I will play inside the house.
Tomorrow will be sunny.

✌ 우리말을 확인하고

너는 검은 구름이 보이니?

오후에는 비가 올 거야.

나는 집 안에서 놀 거야.

내일은 맑을 거야.

✌ 문장을 쓰며 다시 읽기

우리는 공원에 갈 수 있어.
숨바꼭질을 하자.
화요일부터 금요일까지 눈이 올 거야.
장갑과 목도리를 껴야 해.
눈에서 신나게 놀자.

→ We ____can go to the park____ .

→ Let's ____play hide and seek____ .

→ From Tuesday to Friday, it _____ .

→ ____Wear gloves and a scarf____ .

→ Let's ____have fun in the snow____ .

75

Unit 13~14 Review

A 그림을 보고 알맞은 단어를 찾아 쓰세요.

forget
late
wake up

forget

bring
umbrella
put on

dark
cloud
afternoon

fun
inside
hide and seek

B 그림을 보고 알맞은 단어를 찾아 동그라미 하세요.

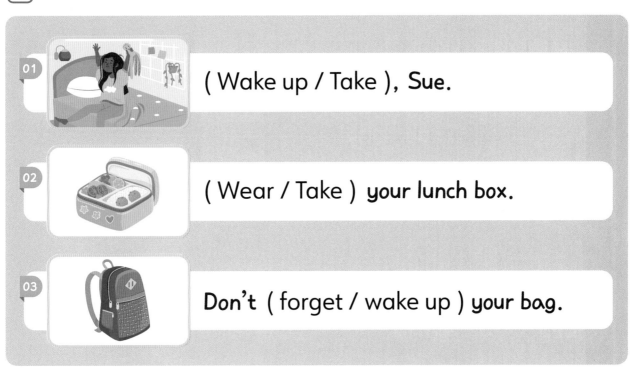

01 (Wake up / Take), Sue.

02 (Wear / Take) your lunch box.

03 Don't (forget / wake up) your bag.

C 그림을 보고 순서에 맞게 써서 문장을 완성하세요.

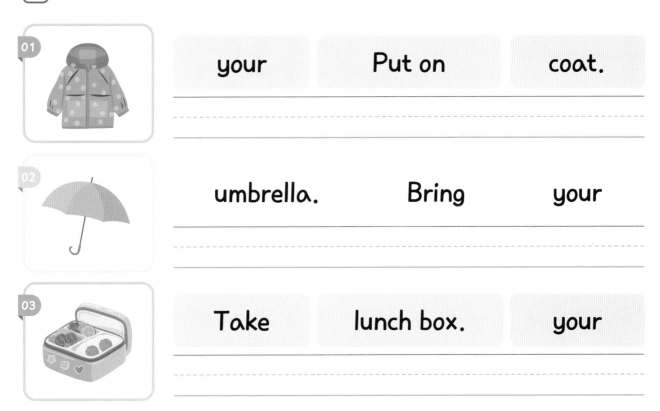

01 your　Put on　coat.

02 umbrella.　Bring　your

03 Take　lunch box.　your

77

문장을 완성하는 데 필요한 단어를 찾아 연결하세요.

01 It _____ in the afternoon. 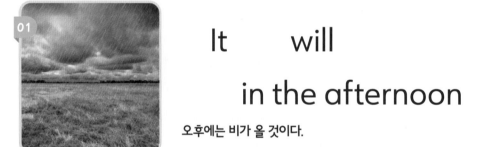 • • will snow

02 I _____ inside the house. • • will play

03 It _____ from Tuesday to Friday. • • will rain

E 그림을 보고 우리말에 맞게 문장을 완성하세요.

01 It   will

_____ in the afternoon   .

오후에는 비가 올 것이다.

02 It

_____ from Tuesday to Friday .

화요일부터 금요일까지 눈이 올 것이다.

03 I

_____ inside the house   .

나는 집 안에서 놀 것이다.

Reading Starter ❷

Dictation

다음을 듣고 빈칸에 알맞은 말을 써 보세요.

Guess Who

I have a _____ tummy.

I have two body parts.

I have eight _____ .

I have _____ .

I have blue blood.

I don't have _____ .

I eat flies.

Be careful. I can bite you.

Who am I?

다음을 듣고 빈칸에 알맞은 말을 써 보세요.

In My Bag

This is my bag.

_____ is a pen in my bag.

There are two _____ in my bag.

There is a water _____ in my bag.

There _____ three books in my bag.

There is a ball in my bag.

There are four _____ in my bag.

What do you have in your bag?

QR코드

다음을 듣고 빈칸에 알맞은 말을 써 보세요.

I Am a Cook

I cook dinner.

Oh, no.

It _____ too salty.

I bake bread.

Oh, no.

It _____ burnt.

I make soup.

Oh, no.

It _____ bad.

A : Don't worry, Matt.

   We can eat _____ .

다음을 듣고 빈칸에 알맞은 말을 써 보세요.

I Can Do

I am grown up now.
I am not a baby.

I can _____ my bed.
I can wash my _____.
I can eat vagetables.

I can _____ my mom.
I can set the _____.
I can _____ the dishes.

Oh, my.
I can't do everything well.

다음을 듣고 빈칸에 알맞은 말을 써 보세요.

Where Is It?

Mom : It's snowing _____ !

Josh : Mom, where is my coat?

Mom : It is _____ the bed.

Josh : Where are my gloves?

Mom : They are in your _____ .

Mom : Where is your _____ ?

Josh : It is _____ the tree.

Mom : Josh! Where are your buttons?

Josh : They are on the snowman.

다음을 듣고 빈칸에 알맞은 말을 써 보세요.

His Job

Tim has a _____ job.

He is a police officer.

He wears a _____ uniform.

He _____ at the police station.

Tim always helps people.

Today, a _____ girl needs his help.

He finds her dog.

She is very _____ with his help.

He is her superhero.

다음을 듣고 빈칸에 알맞은 말을 써 보세요.

Sports and Music

My friends play sports every evening.

Mia _____ soccer.

Jack plays baseball.

Sue plays _____ .

My family has music time every evening.

My dad plays _____ .

My mom plays the violin.

My sister _____ the cello.

I love reading books.

I do not like sports or music.

다음을 듣고 빈칸에 알맞은 말을 써 보세요.

Go Camping

Ella goes _____ with her mom
and dad.

She _____ biking
and catches a butterfly.

Her dad goes _____
and catches a fish.

Her mom goes _____
and sees clouds.

At night, they sit by the fire.

They go _____ at the sky
and see the stars.

QR코드

다음을 듣고 빈칸에 알맞은 말을 써 보세요.

Do You Like Snow?

Jane : Snow is falling from the sky.

          _____ you like snow, Matt?

Matt : _____, I do.

          I like to play in the snow.

Jane : How about rain?

          Do you _____ rain?

Matt : No, I don't. It is too _____

          outside.

          But I like rainbows.

          Do you like _____?

Jane : Yes, I do. They are so _____.

Matt : I love the colors.

다음을 듣고 빈칸에 알맞은 말을 써 보세요.

Does It Have Wings?

Jane : It's time for a quiz.

Matt : _____ it have wings?

Jane : Yes, it does.

It has black and white _____ .

Matt : Does it _____ ?

Jane : No, it doesn't.

Matt : Does _____ well?

Jane : Yes. It swims with its wings.

Matt : Does it _____ in a cold place?

Jane : Yes, it does.

Do you know what it is?

다음을 듣고 빈칸에 알맞은 말을 써 보세요.

My Little Brother

I go to school.

My brother _____ go to school.

I do my homework.

He does not _____ his homework.

I clean my room.

He does not _____ his room.

My _____ takes my toys.

He eats my snacks.

I like him.

But I am not happy with him.

QR코드

다음을 듣고 빈칸에 알맞은 말을 써 보세요.

What Are You Doing?

Today is Sunday.

Dad is in the kitchen.

He is _____ lunch.

Mom is in the living room.

She _____ TV.

My sister is in the bathroom.

She is _____ a dog.

I am in my room.

I am _____ a book.

I am not sleeping.

I am busy, too.

다음을 듣고 빈칸에 알맞은 말을 써 보세요.

Go to School

It is 7 o'clock.

_____ up, Sue.

It is too late.

Take your lunch box.

Don't _____ your bag.

It is cold outside.

_____ your coat.

Oh, my. It is raining.

_____ your umbrella.

QR코드

다음을 듣고 빈칸에 알맞은 말을 써 보세요.

The Weather

Do you see the ⬚⬚⬚⬚⬚ clouds?
It will ⬚⬚⬚⬚⬚ in the afternoon.
I will play inside the house.

Tomorrow ⬚⬚⬚⬚⬚ ⬚⬚⬚⬚⬚ sunny.
We can go to the park.
Let's ⬚⬚⬚⬚⬚ hide and seek.

From Tuesday to Friday, it will ⬚⬚⬚⬚⬚.
Wear gloves and a scarf.
Let's have fun in the snow.

정답 찾아보기

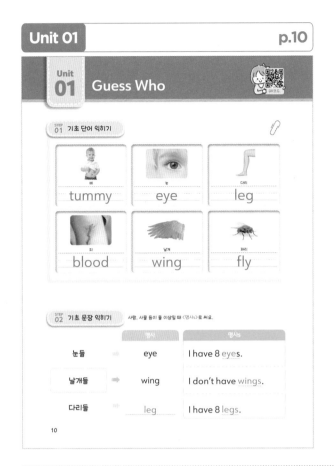

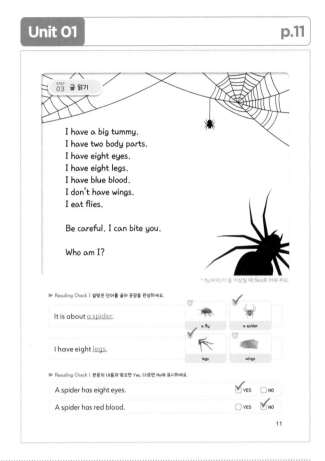

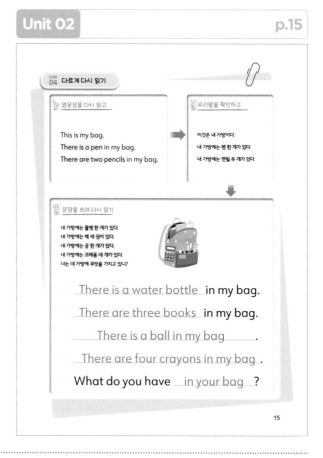

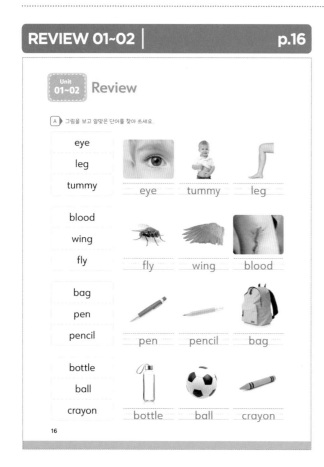

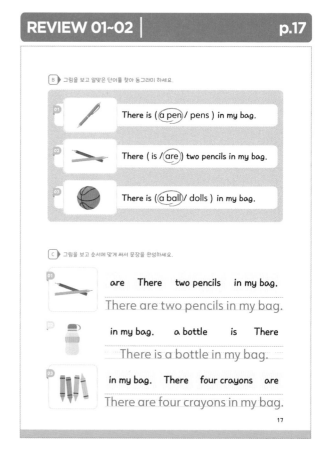

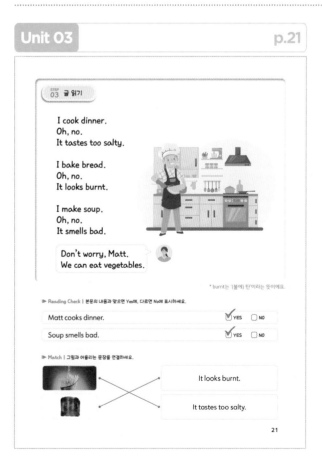

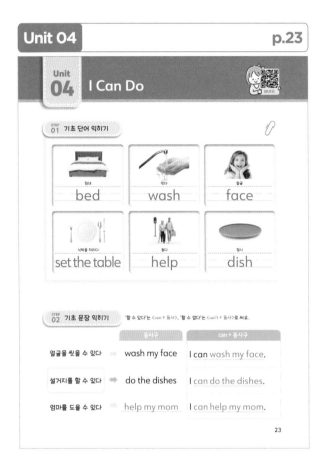

98

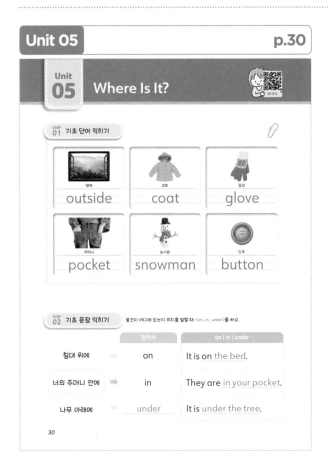

100

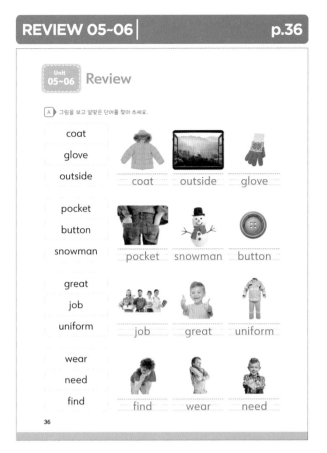

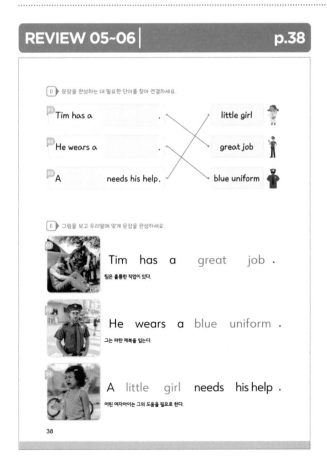

STEP 04 다르게 다시 읽기

✌ 영문장을 다시 읽고

Ella goes camping with her mom and dad.
She goes biking and catches a butterfly.
Her dad goes fishing and catches a fish.

✌ 우리말을 확인하고

엘라는 그녀의 엄마, 아빠와 야영하러 간다.
그녀는 자전거 타러 가고 나비를 잡는다.
그녀의 아빠는 낚시하러 가고 물고기를 잡는다.

✌ 문장을 쓰며 다시 읽기

그녀의 엄마는 하이킹하러 가고 구름을 본다.
밤에 그들은 불 옆에 앉는다.
그들은 하늘을 보러 가고 별을 본다.

Her mom ____ goes hiking ____
and ____ sees clouds ____.

At night, they ____ sit by the fire ____.

They ____ go looking at ____ the sky
and ____ see the stars ____.

45

Unit 07~08 Review

A 그림을 보고 알맞은 단어를 찾아 쓰세요.

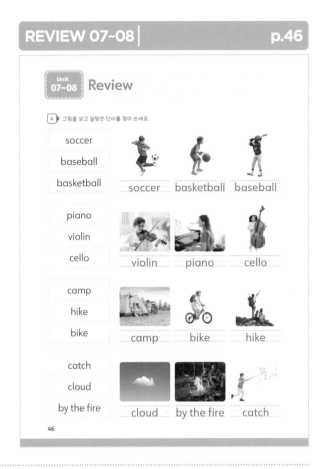

soccer
baseball
basketball

soccer   basketball   baseball

piano
violin
cello

violin   piano   cello

camp
hike
bike

camp   bike   hike

catch
cloud
by the fire

cloud   by the fire   catch

46

B 그림을 보고 알맞은 단어를 찾아 동그라미 하세요.

01 Mia plays ((soccer) / baseball).

02 Sue plays (baseball / (basketball)).

03 My mom plays ((the violin) / cello).

C 그림을 보고 순서에 맞게 써서 문장을 완성하세요.

01 plays   Jack   baseball.
Jack plays baseball.

02 the piano.   My dad   plays
My dad plays the piano.

03 My sister   the cello.   plays
My sister plays the cello.

47

D 문장을 완성하는데 필요한 단어를 찾아 연결하세요.

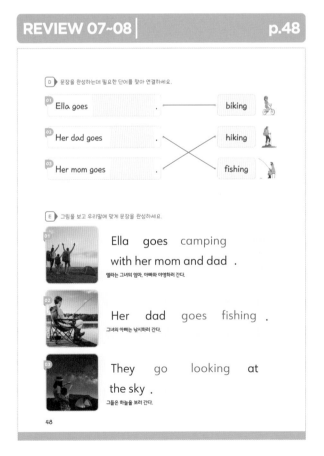

01 Ella goes ____.   biking

02 Her dad goes ____.   hiking

03 Her mom goes ____.   fishing

E 그림을 보고 우리말에 맞게 문장을 완성하세요.

01 Ella goes camping with her mom and dad.
엘라는 그녀의 엄마, 아빠와 야영하러 간다.

02 Her dad goes fishing.
그녀의 아빠는 낚시하러 간다.

03 They go looking at the sky.
그들은 하늘을 보러 간다.

48

103

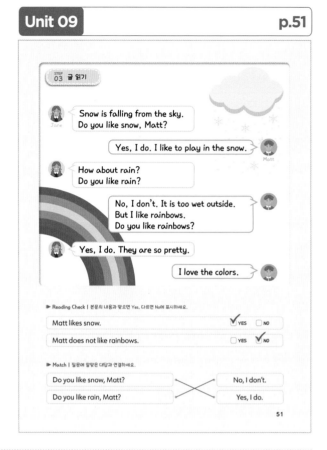

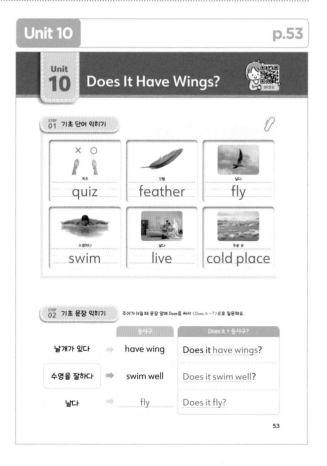

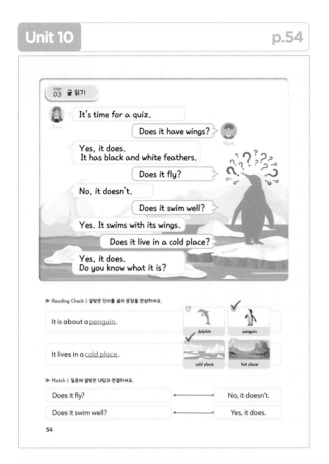

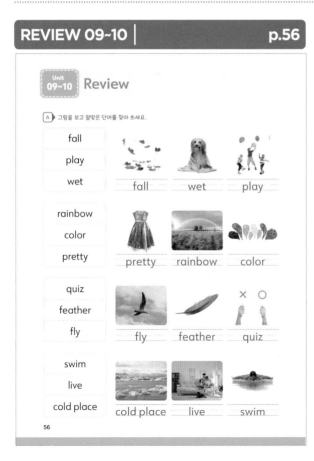

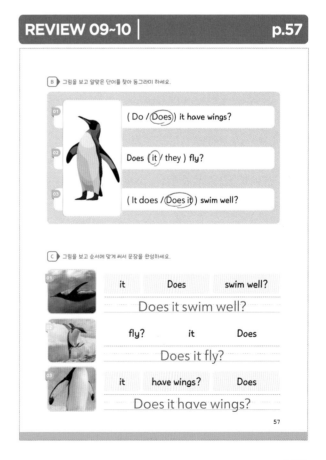

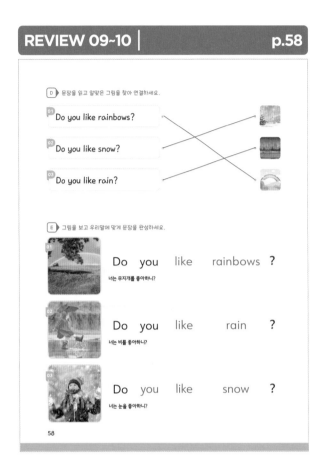

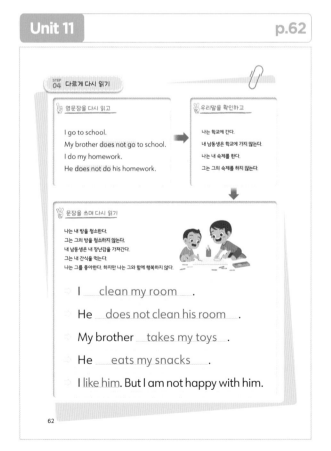

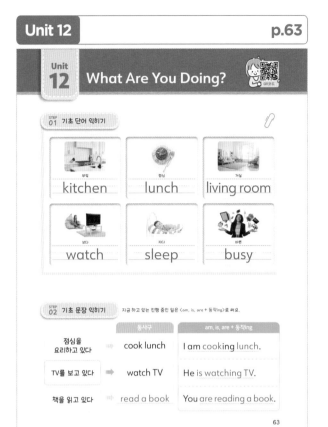

Unit 12 What Are You Doing?

STEP 01 기초 단어 익히기

부엌 kitchen	점심 lunch	거실 living room
보다 watch	자다 sleep	바쁜 busy

STEP 02 기초 문장 익히기   지금 하고 있는 진행 중인 일은 〈am, is, are + 동작ing〉로 써요.

	동사구	am, is, are + 동작ing
점심을 요리하고 있다	cook lunch	I am cooking lunch.
TV를 보고 있다	watch TV	He is watching TV.
책을 읽고 있다	read a book	You are reading a book.

63

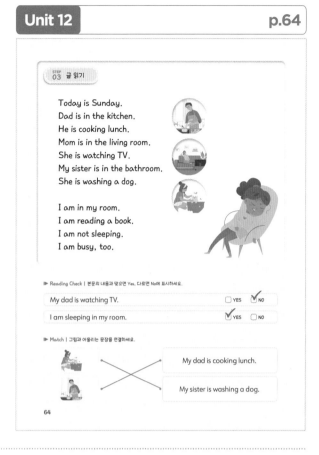

STEP 03 글 읽기

Today is Sunday.
Dad is in the kitchen.
He is cooking lunch.
Mom is in the living room.
She is watching TV.
My sister is in the bathroom.
She is washing a dog.

I am in my room.
I am reading a book.
I am not sleeping.
I am busy, too.

▶ Reading Check | 본문의 내용과 맞으면 Yes, 다르면 No에 표시하세요.

My dad is watching TV.	☐ YES	✓ NO
I am sleeping in my room.	✓ YES	☐ NO

▶ Match | 그림과 어울리는 문장을 연결하세요.

My dad is cooking lunch.

My sister is washing a dog.

64

STEP 04 다르게 다시 읽기

📖 영문장을 다시 읽고

Today is Sunday.
Dad is in the kitchen.
He is cooking lunch.
Mom is in the living room.
She is watching TV.

🐰 우리말을 확인하고

오늘은 일요일이다.
아빠는 부엌에 있다.
그는 점심을 요리하고 있다.
엄마는 거실에 있다.
그녀는 TV를 보고 있다.

✍ 문장을 쓰며 다시 읽기

내 여동생은 욕실에 있다.
그녀는 개를 씻기고 있다.
나는 내 방에 있다.
나는 책을 읽고 있다.
나는 자고 있지 않다. 나도 바쁘다.

My sister   is in the bathroom   .

She   is washing a dog   .

I   am in my room   .

I   am reading a book   .

I am not sleeping. I am busy, too.

65

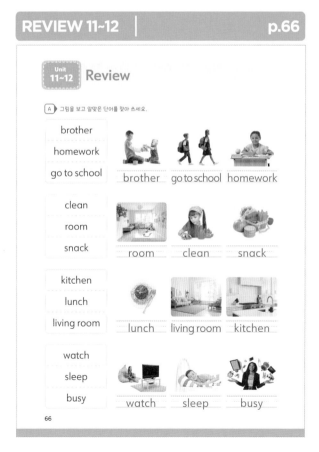

Unit 11~12 Review

Ⓐ 그림을 보고 알맞은 단어를 찾아 쓰세요.

brother homework go to school			
	brother	go to school	homework

clean room snack			
	room	clean	snack

kitchen lunch living room			
	lunch	living room	kitchen

watch sleep busy			
	watch	sleep	busy

66

107

B 그림을 보고 알맞은 단어를 찾아 동그라미 하세요.

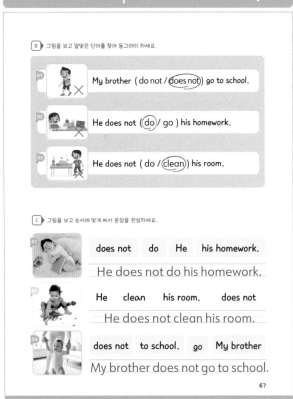

01 My brother (do not / (does not)) go to school.

02 He does not ((do) / go) his homework.

03 He does not (do / (clean)) his room.

C 그림을 보고 순서에 맞게 써서 문장을 완성하세요.

01 does not · do · He · his homework.
He does not do his homework.

02 He · clean · his room. · does not
He does not clean his room.

03 does not · to school. · go · My brother
My brother does not go to school.

67

D 문장을 완성하는 데 필요한 단어를 찾아 연결하세요.

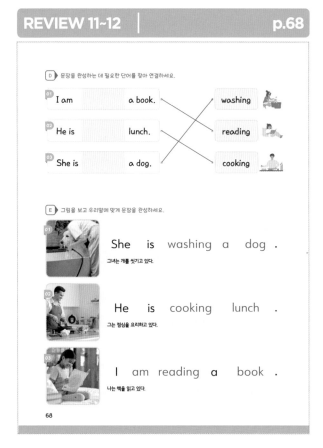

01 I am ___ a book. — washing
02 He is ___ lunch. — reading
03 She is ___ a dog. — cooking

E 그림을 보고 우리말에 맞게 문장을 완성하세요.

01 She is washing a dog .
그녀는 개를 씻기고 있다.

02 He is cooking lunch .
그는 점심을 요리하고 있다.

03 I am reading a book .
나는 책을 읽고 있다.

68

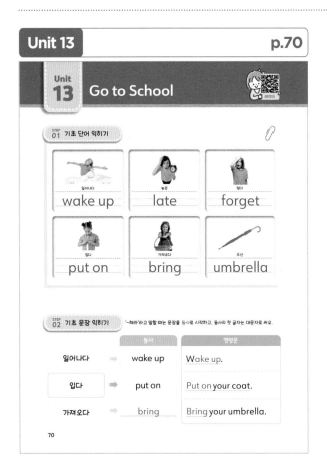

Unit 13 Go to School

STEP 01 기초 단어 익히기

wake up · late · forget
put on · bring · umbrella

STEP 02 기초 문장 익히기

일어나다 → wake up → Wake up.
입다 → put on → Put on your coat.
가져오다 → bring → Bring your umbrella.

70

STEP 03 글 읽기

It is 7 o'clock.
Wake up, Sue.
It is too late.
Take your lunch box.
Don't forget your bag.

It is cold outside.
Put on your coat.
Oh, my. It is raining.
Bring your umbrella.

Reading Check

It is a rainy day. ☑YES ☐NO
Sue forgets her bag. ☐YES ☑NO

Match

umbrella — Take your lunch box.
lunch box — Bring your umbrella.

71

108

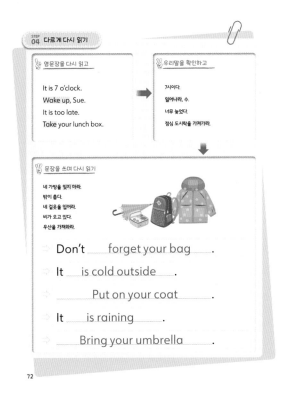

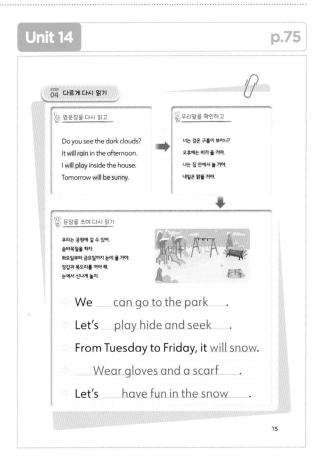

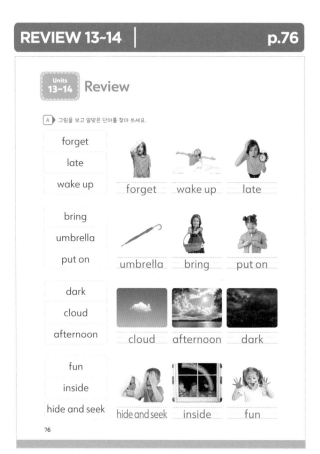

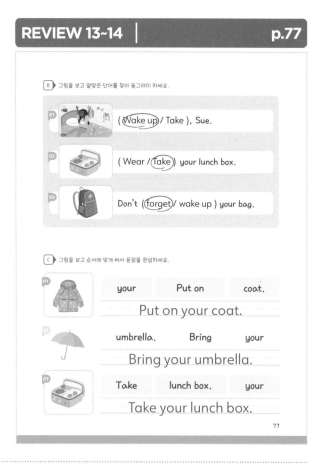

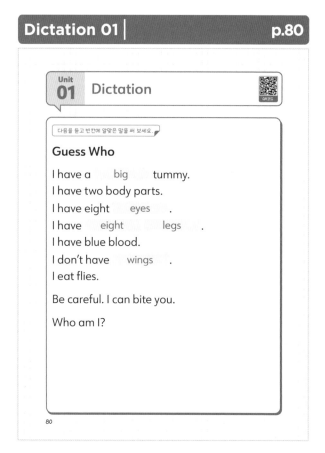

Unit 02 Dictation

다음을 듣고 빈칸에 알맞은 말을 써 보세요.

In My Bag

This is my bag.

__There__ is a pen in my bag.

There are two __pencils__ in my bag.

There is a water __bottle__ in my bag.

There __are__ three books in my bag.

There is a ball in my bag.

There are four __crayons__ in my bag.

What do you have in your bag?

81

Unit 03 Dictation

다음을 듣고 빈칸에 알맞은 말을 써 보세요.

I Am a Cook

I cook dinner.

Oh, no.

It __tastes__ too salty.

I bake bread.

Oh, no.

It __looks__ burnt.

I make soup.

Oh, no.

It __smells__ bad.

A : Don't worry, Matt.

We can eat __vegetables__ .

82

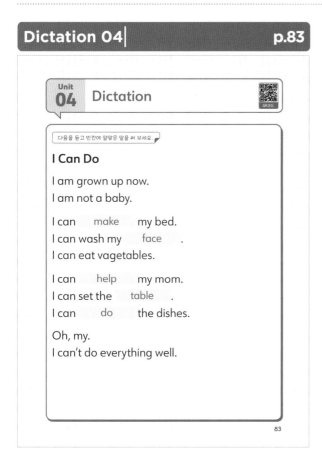

Unit 04 Dictation

다음을 듣고 빈칸에 알맞은 말을 써 보세요.

I Can Do

I am grown up now.

I am not a baby.

I can __make__ my bed.

I can wash my __face__ .

I can eat vagetables.

I can __help__ my mom.

I can set the __table__ .

I can __do__ the dishes.

Oh, my.

I can't do everything well.

83

Unit 05 Dictation

다음을 듣고 빈칸에 알맞은 말을 써 보세요.

Where Is It?

Mom : It's snowing __outside__ !

Josh : Mom, where is my coat?

Mom : It is __on__ the bed.

Josh : Where are my gloves?

Mom : They are in your __pocket__ .

Mom : Where is your __snowman__ ?

Josh : It is __under__ the tree.

Mom : Josh! Where are your buttons?

Josh : They are on the snowman.

84

111

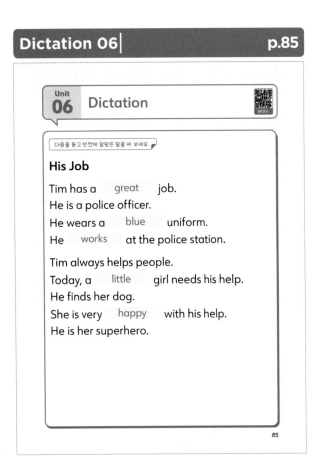

Unit 06 Dictation

다음을 듣고 빈칸에 알맞은 말을 써 보세요.

His Job

Tim has a great job.
He is a police officer.
He wears a blue uniform.
He works at the police station.

Tim always helps people.
Today, a little girl needs his help.
He finds her dog.
She is very happy with his help.
He is her superhero.

85

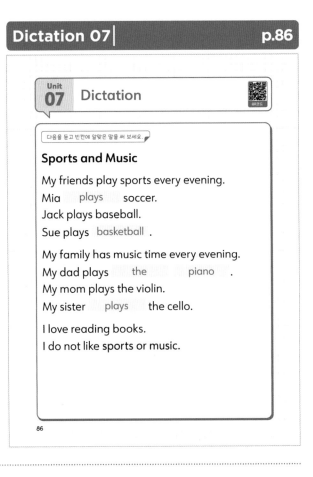

Unit 07 Dictation

다음을 듣고 빈칸에 알맞은 말을 써 보세요.

Sports and Music

My friends play sports every evening.
Mia plays soccer.
Jack plays baseball.
Sue plays basketball .

My family has music time every evening.
My dad plays the piano .
My mom plays the violin.
My sister plays the cello.

I love reading books.
I do not like **sports** or **music**.

86

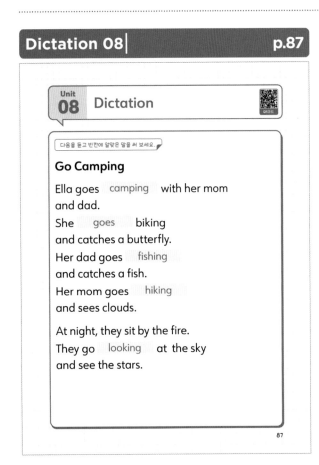

Unit 08 Dictation

다음을 듣고 빈칸에 알맞은 말을 써 보세요.

Go Camping

Ella goes camping with her mom
and dad.
She goes biking
and catches a butterfly.
Her dad goes fishing
and catches a fish.
Her mom goes hiking
and sees clouds.

At night, they sit by the fire.
They go looking at the sky
and see the stars.

87

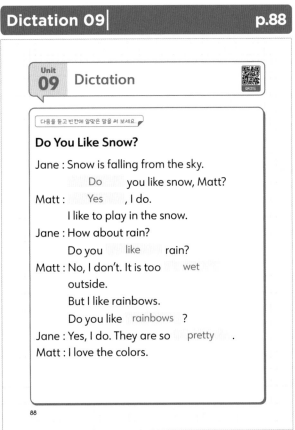

Unit 09 Dictation

다음을 듣고 빈칸에 알맞은 말을 써 보세요.

Do You Like Snow?

Jane : Snow is falling from the sky.
        Do you like snow, Matt?
Matt : Yes , I do.
        I like to play in the snow.
Jane : How about rain?
        Do you like rain?
Matt : No, I don't. It is too wet
        outside.
        But I like rainbows.
        Do you like rainbows ?
Jane : Yes, I do. They are so pretty .
Matt : I love the colors.

88

Dictation 10 | p.89

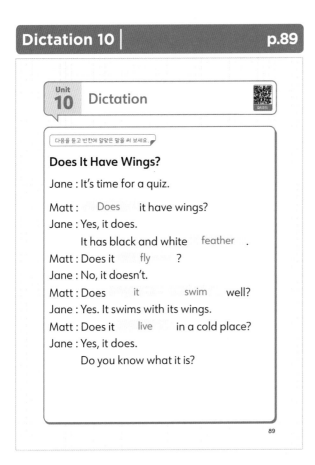

Unit 10 Dictation

다음을 듣고 빈칸에 알맞은 말을 써 보세요.

Does It Have Wings?

Jane : It's time for a quiz.

Matt : **Does** it have wings?
Jane : Yes, it does.
It has black and white **feather** .
Matt : Does it **fly** ?
Jane : No, it doesn't.
Matt : Does **it** **swim** well?
Jane : Yes. It swims with its wings.
Matt : Does it **live** in a cold place?
Jane : Yes, it does.
Do you know what it is?

89

Dictation 11 | p.90

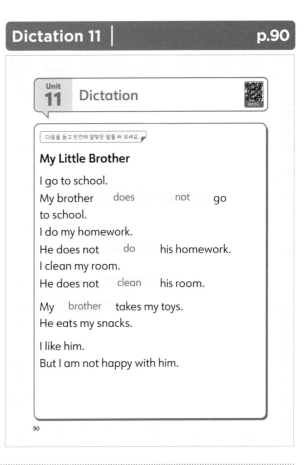

Unit 11 Dictation

다음을 듣고 빈칸에 알맞은 말을 써 보세요.

My Little Brother

I go to school.
My brother **does** **not** **go** to school.
I do my homework.
He does not **do** his homework.
I clean my room.
He does not **clean** his room.

My **brother** takes my toys.
He eats my snacks.

I like him.
But I am not happy with him.

90

Dictation 12 | p.91

Unit 12 Dictation

다음을 듣고 빈칸에 알맞은 말을 써 보세요.

What Are You Doing?

Today is Sunday.
Dad is in the kitchen.
He is **cooking** lunch.
Mom is in the living room.
She **is** **watching** TV.
My sister is in the bathroom.
She is **washing** a dog.

I am in my room.
I am **reading** a book.
I am not sleeping.
I am busy, too.

91

Dictation 13 | p.92

Unit 13 Dictation

다음을 듣고 빈칸에 알맞은 말을 써 보세요.

Go to School

It is 7 o'clock.
Wake up, Sue.
It is too late.
Take your lunch box.
Don't **forget** your bag.

It is cold outside.
Put **on** your coat.
Oh, my. It is raining.
Bring your umbrella.

92

113

14 Dictation

다음을 듣고 빈칸에 알맞은 말을 써 보세요.

The Weather

Do you see the   dark   clouds?
It will   rain   in the afternoon.
I will play inside the house.

Tomorrow   will   be   sunny.
We can go to the park.
Let's   play   hide and seek.

From Tuesday to Friday, it will   snow   .
Wear gloves and a scarf.
Let's have fun in the snow.

93

114

'공부 습관'이야말로 가장 큰 재능입니다.
재능많은영어연구소는 최고의 학습 효과를 내는
최적의 학습 플랜을 고민합니다.

소장 윤미영

경희대학교 영문학과와 같은 대학에서 석사학위를 받았습니다. 20여 년 동안 지학사, 디딤돌, 키 영어학습방법연구소, 롱테일 교육연구소에서 초등생과 중고생을 위한 영어 교재를 기획하고 만드는 일을 해 왔습니다. 베스트셀러인《문법이 쓰기다》,《단어가 읽기다》,《구문이 독해다》, 혼공 시리즈《혼공 초등 영단어》,《혼공 초등 영문법》, 바빠시리즈의《바빠 초등 필수 영단어》등을 집필했습니다.

초등영어 읽기독립 리딩 스타터 2

1판 1쇄 발행일 2024년 5월 13일

지은이 재능많은영어연구소

발행인 김학원
발행처 휴먼어린이
출판등록 제313-2006-000161호(2006년 7월 31일)
주소 (03991) 서울시 마포구 동교로23길 76(연남동)
전화 02-335-4422 **팩스** 02-334-3427
저자·독자 서비스 humanist@humanistbooks.com
홈페이지 www.humanistbooks.com
유튜브 youtube.com/user/humanistma **포스트** post.naver.com/hmcv
페이스북 facebook.com/hmcv2001 **인스타그램** @human_kids

편집주간 황서현 **편집** 이서현 **원어민 검토** Sherwood Choe
표지 디자인 유주현 **본문 디자인** PRISM C **음원 제작** 109Sound
용지 화인페이퍼 **인쇄** 삼조인쇄 **제본** 해피문화사

ⓒ 재능많은영어연구소·윤미영, 2024

ISBN 978-89-6591-581-2 64740
ISBN 978-89-6591-576-8 64740(세트)